QUESTIONS: SIKHS

It is possible to characterise the Sikh faith as a search for truth and truthful living. This search for truth includes looking within, to reflect on the human condition, as well as looking outward, towards the Infinite. But Guru Nanak emphasised that how a Sikh lives is even more important: 'Truth is high, but higher still is truthful living' (Guru Nanak, Adi Granth 62).

Early on the opening page of the Guru Granth Sahib, Guru Nanak asks the first question of the Sikh scriptures: 'How can one become truthful?' (AG 1). This process of becoming truthful is at the heart of Sikh living; the belief in Truth is expressed through the practice of truthful living. So, belief in the equality of all people is expressed in the rejection of caste discrimination, which then leads to the practice of sewa (selfless service). The belief that there are no intermediaries between human beings and God is expressed in the rejection of priestly ritual.

Sikhs are encouraged to work hard for a living. This belief in honest living as a path to God is itself balanced by the acknowledgement that Sikhs rely upon the grace of God in their search for Truth.

Questions: Sikh  beliefs and Sikh section outline for Sikhs and these beliefs everyday living

There are cla activities to enable students to explore the Sikh search for Truth, through examining the experience of Guru Nanak and the words of the Mool Mantar (pp.12–18). The search for truthful living is explored through Sikh architecture and values (pp.5–11), and by applying Sikh teachings from the Guru Granth Sahib to daily living (pp.19–24). Interviews with four teenagers in the UK reveal the impact of their Sikh faith on their lives, with a particular focus on becoming khalsa Sikhs (pp.25–31).

As with all the books in this series, the activities integrate learning about religion and learning from religion, supporting students in the development of their understanding of Sikhism and in examination of their own experiences in the light of this understanding. Creative activities can help to promote interpretive skills, critical analysis and reflective thinking – all important in the student's own search for truth and truthful living.

Stephen Pett
Editor

Contents

A view from inside Sikhism Opinderjit Kaur Takhar	2
Visual learning: How can Sikh architecture reveal Sikh values? Lat Blaylock	5
How and why do Sikhs remember God? Rosemary Rivett	12
What do Sikhs believe about how you should live? Stephen Pett	19
What does it mean to be a young Sikh in Britain today? Fiona Moss	25
Access and Challenge Lat Blaylock	32

A VIEW FROM INSIDE SIKHISM

As part of our series from faith communities, Dr Opinderjit Kaur Takhar here answers some questions about Sikhism, or Sikhi, as many prefer. Formerly an RE teacher and now Head of Religious Studies at the University of Wolverhampton, Opinderjit has published widely on Sikhism and offers an authentic and informative insider voice.

Dr Kaur Opinderjit Kaur Takhar

What do you want young people to know about Sikhism in Britain today?

Sikhism is the youngest of the world religions but the fifth largest in the world. According to the 2011 Census, there are 423,000 Sikhs in Britain, making up 0.8 per cent of the total population of England and Wales. Many Sikhs prefer the term *Sikhi* instead of Sikhism to show that this faith is not just about a system of belief, it is a path to follow, a way of life. The term 'Sikh' comes from the word *sikhna* which means 'to learn': hence a Sikh is a learner.

The Guru Granth Sahib uniquely contains both the words of the Sikh gurus and hymns from Hindu and Muslim Sants (holy individuals).

In the *Janamsakhis* (birth testimonies of Guru Nanak), Guru Nanak said: 'There is no Hindu, there is no Muslim, so whose path shall I follow? I shall follow God's path. God is neither Hindu nor Muslim, and the path which I follow is God's'. This indicates the unity of God: that God is beyond all religious divisions. The emphasis is on the liberation of *all* human beings, regardless of caste or faith.

The Sikh place of worship, *gurdwara*, is open to all. The importance of the egalitarian principles of Sikhism is clearly portrayed through the distribution of *karah prasad* and *langar* in the gurdwara. The concept of eating together illustrates that all visitors to the *gurdwara* are equal.

There are three basic tenets of faith to be expressed through one's everyday living according to Sikhi. These are:

1 **Nam Simran:** meditation/recitation on the name of God.
2 **Kirt Karo:** to work hard and earn an honest day's living. Sikhs are encouraged to take part in charitable events.
3 **Vand ke chakko:** to share one's food and earnings with the less fortunate.

What matters most to British Sikhs at the moment?

Sikhs recognise that it is important to be aware of what it means to be a Sikh for the younger generation of Sikhs and the wider British population. Issues and events in the Punjab also affect the Sikh diaspora in countries such as Britain and the USA.

Religious identity associated with the Khalsa is very important to the British Sikh community. Hence active campaigning has successfully taken place since the 1980s to allow Sikhs the right to wear their articles of faith in public. Recently, Jatenderpal Singh Bhullar became the first Royal Guard to wear a turban instead of the traditional bearskin which has been the official headdress for Royal Guards for the last 180 years. The ban on wearing the turban has also been overthrown for Sikhs in France, despite France's secular values.

The concept of tolerance to other faiths is a prominent feature of the teachings of the Sikh Gurus. These teachings, referred to as *gurbani*, are contained in the Sikh holy scripture, the Guru Granth Sahib. Many Sikhs, true to the essence of gurbani, are much involved in interfaith matters in Britain and across the globe. The teachings of Guru Nanak further support his pioneering interfaith attitudes.

What are the issues that concern the Sikh community?

Sikhs are worried about the decline in attendance at the gurdwara of the younger generation. A great deal of work is being done to encourage youngsters to take an active role in the running of activities at the gurdwaras. There is a linked concern about the survival of the Punjabi language in the diaspora Sikh communities.

Significant numbers of Sikhs living and born in Britain are linked to one political movement or another. Some of these political parties are pro-Khalistani. Khalistan is the demand for a separatist Sikh state, autonomous in terms of severing authority from the central Indian government. Strongly linked in with this separatist insurgency are the events of Operation Bluestar and the aftermath of the assassination of Indira Gandhi in 1984.

It is incorrect to assume, however, that all Sikhs are in favour of Khalistan. Many Sikhs are actively campaigning for the Indian government to accept that it turned a blind eye to the mass genocide of Sikhs in Delhi in the aftermath of 1984, hence the oft-repeated slogan 'never forget 84'. These Sikhs, however, are not necessarily also campaigning for Khalistan.

Equality among all human beings is a central tenet of the egalitarian spirit of the Sikh faith. Sikh teachings emphasise that the essence of the Divine is immanent in the hearts of all human beings; this in turn entails that all human beings are equal. Thus, Sikhi rejects any form of caste- or gender-based discrimination. Increasingly, Sikh feminists are challenging male-dominated hegemony amongst the Sikhs. Caste-based gurdwaras are also being criticised on the grounds that they are contradicting the essential message of egalitarianism.

Do you have a favourite story that means a lot to you? What is it and why does it matter?

A story that I find particularly inspiring is that of Bhai Lalo and Malik Bhago. The principle of Kirt Karo (honest livelihood) is beautifully emphasised in this story.

The narrative tells of how Guru Nanak, while on his travels, passed through a place known as Saidpur and decided to stay with a poor carpenter, Bhai Lalo. On hearing that Guru Nanak was staying with Bhai Lalo, a rich but corrupt landlord named Malik Bhago invited him to dinner. Bhago had made his money through the exploitation of farmers, who lived in poverty and hunger due to the high taxes that he charged them for cultivating the land. Guru Nanak declined Malik Bhago's invitation to dinner.

The angry Bhago demanded that Guru Nanak visit his home and explain why he declined the offer of a lavish banquet as compared to the simple food offered by a poor man, Lalo. Guru Nanak replied that he could not possibly eat food that had been made with money obtained from exploiting poor workers. He said he would rather eat Lalo's food since it was made from money earned by an honest day's work.

To prove his point, Guru Nanak squeezed a chapatti (flat bread) from Bhago's meal in one hand and one from Lalo's in the other. Blood dripped from Bhago's chapatti whilst milk dripped from Lalo's chapatti. Bhago was guilt-ridden and asked for Guru Nanak's forgiveness by agreeing to share his wealth with the poor.

This story is a fine example of the emphasis that the Sikh faith places on honest hard work.

What issues do you want RE teachers to remember when they plan to teach about Sikhism?

1. **Sikhi is diverse:** Teaching should address diversity in Sikh beliefs and practices. Sikhs are not a monolithic community and such textbook representations should be avoided. In similar fashion to all faith communities, there are sectarian divisions among Sikhs. It is worthwhile being aware of the efforts of the Singh Sabha movement (later becoming the Tat Khalsa) from 1873 CE onwards in its attempts at establishing a monolithic and hegemonic Sikh identity.

   Some groups within the Panth are viewed as highly controversial due to their beliefs. One such tradition is that of the Namdharis who continue the line of human Gurus beyond Guru Gobind Singh. Other groups include the Valmikis, Ravidassias and Sant Nirankaris. There are a number of opinions as to whether such groups should be regarded as Sikhs.

2. **Sikh identity is complex:** In terms of appearance, not all Sikhs who wear a turban and the 5Ks are *amritdhari* (initiated). Many Sikhs are *kesdhari* (they do not cut their hair or beard) without necessarily being amritdhari. There are also significant numbers of Sikhs who cut their hair and may be labelled as *mona* or *sahajdhari*. A number of Sikhs will refer to an amritdhari as the ideal Sikh, although this is not strictly speaking in line with the teachings of the Guru Granth Sahib.

3. **The relation of culture to faith:** Addressing cultural as well as religious practices will also aid the teacher in addressing issues of diversity amongst Sikhs. The Punjabi norm of endogamy (marrying within one's caste) is significantly followed among many Sikhs. Importantly, however, this is being challenged by the more educated and younger generation of Sikhs as going against the egalitarian nature of Sikhi. The presence of caste amongst Sikhs is a controversial topic and should be approached with sensitivity. It is appropriate to refer to marriages within the British Sikh community as being *assisted* rather than arranged. So-called 'love' marriages are also becoming widely accepted.

4. **Meet some Sikhs!** Visiting the gurdwara is essential when planning to teach about the Sikh faith. Sikhi is a vibrant and colourful way of life for millions of followers. Teachers should explore this aspect in their teaching by developing strong links, if possible, with their local Sikh gurdwaras. Sikhs are well known for their hospitality, and gurdwaras welcome visitors all the time.

 An extended version of this interview is available online to subscribers. More than double the length of the printed article, it is an indispensable guide to Sikhi.

 Activities for your highest-achieving students, using this interview, can be found on p.33.

What matters to Sikhs? What matters to me?

The interview with Opinderjit Takhar outlines some ideas that are relevant to any study of Sikhism. Use the interview and your own ideas to fill in this grid, giving evidence to back up your answers.

This is/is not important to Sikhs because . . .	Idea/value	This is/is not important to me because . . .
	Meditation on the name of God	
	Hard work and honest living	
	Being generous with those less fortunate than me	
	Equality	
	The caste system	
	Freedom to express my identity	
	Tolerance of different faiths and beliefs	

VISUAL LEARNING: HOW CAN SIKH ARCHITECTURE REVEAL SIKH VALUES?

Summary of learning

This unit of work makes a good introduction to Sikh religion. Many students come fresh to learning from Sikhism at age 11: this might be a good way to begin. Later units in this book will develop students' understanding further.

Using high-quality visual stimulus materials, with good visual learning and thinking skills strategies, this unit enables **students aged 11-13** to enquire into the Sikh architecture of Harmandir Sahib (the 'Golden Temple'). They will be challenged to think about how architecture expresses beliefs and values, and to consider for themselves different ways of expressing what matters most. They will work in small teams to express their own values in an architectural plan.

Websites like Flickr have hundreds of wonderful photos of Harmandir Sahib. Ask students to look for three that they really like, and say why.

Information for the teacher: sacred journey

Some people use the word 'pilgrimage' to describe a sacred journey. Most Sikhs prefer not to talk of a pilgrimage, perhaps partly because Guru Nanak was a sharp critic of religious ritual. Sikhs still visit some significant places in their history to show respect.

Symbolism

Sikhs say that coming to God, who is great, we are all equal.

- There are 13 steps downwards at the entrance to the Golden Temple.
- In your eye line, this makes it look as if the temple is elevating, rising up, as you go down the steps
- The word 'thirteen' in Punjabi means 'yours' – everything belongs to Waheguru (God).

Peace within

- Harmandir Sahib is part of a bustling city – but inside the blue gates, the noise disappears and calm reigns. Sikhs might say that the peace of God can be found when we turn from life's business. Many spiritual people – not just Sikhs – look for a sense of God's presence in silence.

Names and meanings

- 'Harmandir Sahib' is the proper name for the Golden Temple. It means 'house of God – holy'. The normal name of a Sikh place of worship is *gurdwara* – the doorway of the Guru. This refers to the fact that the Guru Granth Sahib, which is not a mere book but is honoured by Sikhs as their living Guru today, is housed in a gurdwara.

Outcomes

Students can show their achievements at levels 3–6 through these activities if they can say 'Yes' to some of these 'I can' statements:

Description of achievement:
I can...

Level 3

- describe simply some features of the Golden Temple
- make a simple link between Sikh beliefs and values and the symbols of equality in the Golden Temple.

Level 4

- use the right words to show that I understand the symbolism of the Golden Temple and its expression of Sikh values
- comment on whether Sikh concepts of equality and service are relevant to me, saying why.

Level 5

- explain the emotional or spiritual impact for Sikhs of visiting Harmandir Sahib
- express my own views of the Sikh idea that ritual actions are of no benefit in reaching God, giving reasons to support my opinions.

Level 6

- interpret the meanings of different aspects of Sikh values and service thoughtfully
- insightfully express my own viewpoint about Sikh teachings and practices in relation to others' views, using reason and argument to back it up.

RE Today Services

Learning activities

Activity 1
Look to learn

Use the copies of the framework on p.7, one for each pair of students. Ask students, in pairs, to raise some questions about the images. Tell them 'big questions' are best – and model some examples: 'Is the cloth mostly red or more blue?' (little question) 'How might someone find God at the Golden Temple?' (big question). Good visual learning can develop enquiring thinking.

When each pair has created questions beginning with most of the key enquiry words, collect the sheets in. Share some knowledge about the Golden Temple, either through Activity 2 or from textbooks and other resources.

Give out the sheets of questions, each to a different pair of students. Ask them to suggest answers to any of the questions they can, and write these onto the reverse side of the sheet. When the papers go back to the original students, they can weigh up whether their classmates gave good answers.

 Copies of the images from p.7 and p.9 are available online for RE Today subscribers to download.

Activity 2
Sequencing

Give each pair or small group of students an envelope with twelve individual cards copied from p.8. Ask them to sort out the cards into the 'right order'. There are several ways of doing this, but lots more that are clearly wrong. The page as it is printed gives one good way of sequencing: the left-hand column gives historical information about the development of Harmandir Sahib; the right-hand column suggests symbols, meanings and significance of the developments.

 For alternative ways in to this unit for lower-achieving students, see p.32.

Activity 3
Enquiry framework

1 Enlarge and copy p.9 on to A3 paper for pairs of students. Ask them to devise 7 to 14 questions about the picture, writing their questions into the left hand boxes. Emphasise to them that good questions go deeper, so the first thing they think of may not be the best question. Give them seven minutes to do this. Collect the sheets in.

2 **Give some information** about the image. This shows Guru Nanak's visit, 500 years ago, to the Muslim holy city of Makkah, the centre of the world for Muslims. He and his companion lay on the ground with their feet pointing towards the holy Ka'ba. This was offensive to some Muslims, who ran to complain. Guru Nanak said he was happy to be moved: 'Please turn me round to a position where my feet do not point towards God.' What sort of answer is that? Puzzling? Clever?

Guru Nanak taught: 'God is not a Muslim. God is not a Hindu. So whose path shall I follow? God's path!'

Ask: what does this show about how much Guru Nanak values: Islam / God / religious ritual / deep thinking / being challenged?

3 **Attempting answers:** Give each pair of students one of the visual questioning sheets from p.9 done by other students. Can they guess, work out or speculate some answers? Ask them to discuss carefully before putting pen to paper. Display the A3 sheets round the classroom, and ask students to walk and look at all the questions and answers that were asked. This learning strategy emphasises to students that they can learn from each other's ideas and answers.

4 **Did you learn ten things?** Give students, individually or in pairs, a copy of the picture to stick in the centre of a piece of paper. They are to annotate their picture with at least ten things they have learned about Sikhs. This can be done individually if you need evidence of achievement from this, or in pairs, for increased depth and thoughtfulness.

Activity 4
Reasons PLUS!

Teach students that, in RE, giving an opinion may be step one, but it's not good RE unless you give a reason. Use the visual learning stimulus of the picture of Guru Nanak at Makkah again, and explore the controversy about giving offence that goes with it. Point out to students that they are to build up their skills as arguers.

Using the beautiful painting examined in Activity 3, the table on p.10 gives some provocative statements together with some examples of reasons and arguments – both important parts of RE. Can students come up with some more statements that might add to the arguments here?

Ask students to complete the sentences they agree with first, using 'because' as a connective. Then try the ones they don't agree with. Can they see reasons even for opinions they disagree with? Can students add to the reasons given, deepening them?

Activity 5
Spiritual architects

The activity on p.11 will need a full lesson or even two to allow students to create a successful product. It aims to develop students' understanding about Sikh holy places in comparison with their own sense of the sacred.

Activity 1 Look to learn, raising questions

Look carefully at the two pictures of Harmandir Sahib, called the 'Golden Temple of Amritsar', a sacred building for Sikhs. With your partner, come up with at least eight good questions about the Golden Temple and these two pictures of it.

What . . .

How . . .

Where . . .

Who . . .

Which . . .

How many . . .

What if . . .

Why . . .

Harimandar Sahib: the Golden Temple at Amritsar, c.1840. Collection of Satinder and Narinder Kapany. Used by permission

What . . .

How . . .

Where . . .

Who . . .

Which . . .

How many . . .

What if . . .

Why . . .

One of these is an ancient painting, the other is a wall hanging made in 2010. Which one might be most precious to a Sikh person and why?

© 2013 RE Today Services
Permission is granted to photocopy this page for use in classroom activities in schools that have purchased this publication.

Activity 2 Sequencing

These twelve cards are for sequencing. They give some of the history and symbolism of the Golden Temple.

In 1570 CE, Guru Amar Das asked his successor Guru Ram Das to remake the beautiful lake in Amritsar, creating a holy pool, a 'Sarovar'.	The lake in Amritsar was visited by people seeking healing. The new temple was to be a place of healing and peace for all.
One tradition says that in December 1588 CE Guru Arjan asked Mian Mir, a Muslim saint, to lay the foundation stone of the new temple.	Sikhs have always included the spiritual ideas of Muslims, Hindus and others in their scriptures: there is one Truth, found along many paths.
In 1604 CE Guru Arjan completed Harmandir Sahib (Golden Temple) on a 20m square platform in the lake at Amritsar.	Some temples are built high up on hills. Harmandir Sahib is not – it's on the level of the water. Everyone comes equal to God.
Door frames over 3m tall with beautiful arches above open onto each of the four sides of the Harmandir Sahib.	Come to God from where you are: north, south, east or west, the Golden Temple is open to all. God is found from all directions.
The causeway leading to the Golden Temple across the tank of holy nectar is over 60m long and 6m wide. Over 100,000 people cross the causeway every day.	Everyone comes to the Golden Temple – and to God – over the same causeway. God does not discriminate. God has no prejudice.
Harmandir Sahib became the 'Golden Temple' in the nineteenth century when Maharaja Ranjit Singh had it covered in gold. It was paid for by donations.	Gold symbolises perfection. Sikhs across the world are devoted to the beauty of the teaching of the Gurus: being generous with gold shows this.

© 2013 RE Today Services
Permission is granted to photocopy this page for use in classroom activities in schools that have purchased this publication.

Activity 3 Visual learning from Guru Nanak

Look at the picture and create good questions

Guru Nanak and his disciple encounter a Muslim cleric at Mecca. Gift of the Kapany Collection, 1998.58.23.
© Asian Art Museum of San Fransisco. Used by permission.

- What. . . .
- Who. . . .
- Where. . . .
- How. . . .
- When . . . .
- Which . . . .
- Why . . . .

© 2013 RE Today Services
Permission is granted to photocopy this page for use in classroom activities in schools that have purchased this publication.

Activity 4 Reasons and reasons PLUS!

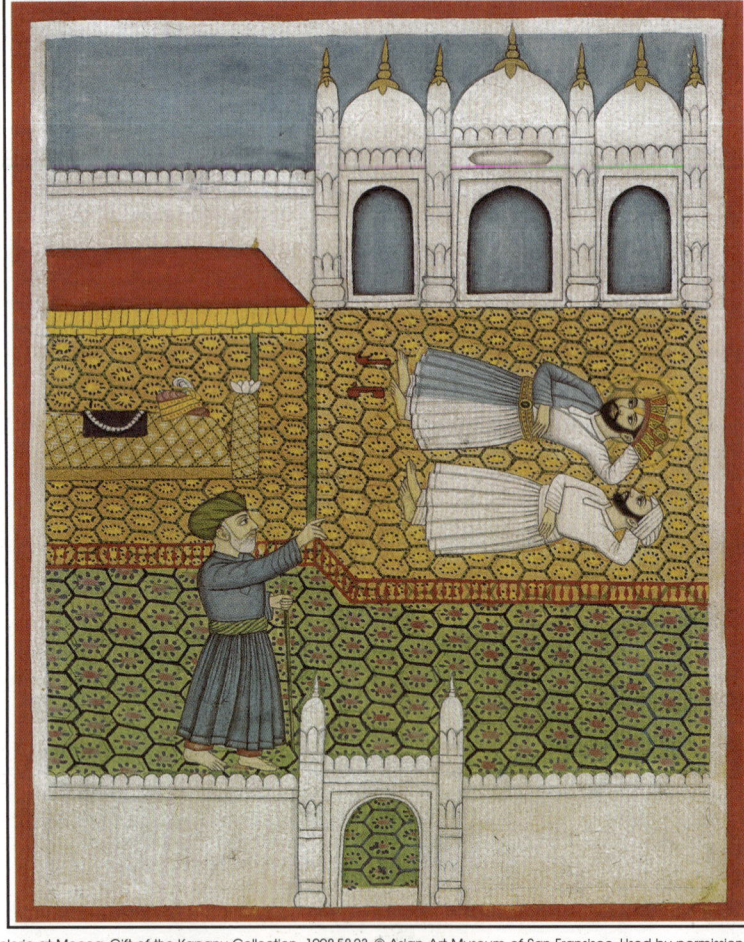

Guru Nanak and his disciple encounter a Muslim cleric at Mecca. Gift of the Kapany Collection, 1998.58.23. © Asian Art Museum of San Fransisco. Used by permission.

Guru Nanak upset a Muslim at Makkah to make a point: God is greater than religion.

| I agree: he proved his point by a subtle action. Muslims also agree with Sikhs here really, because... | He was wrong: he didn't need to risk giving offence. He could have just explained, because... |

If God is real, then 'He' would not care whether you point your feet the wrong way. God would care if you are good, kind, just and loving.

| I agree: rituals don't matter much compared to being good and doing what is right, because... | I disagree. I think religious ritual can support a person in doing good. It makes sense of life, because... |

Sikhs and Muslims both teach belief in one God, so their religions are the same in essence.

| I agree. Belief is at the heart of religion, so a key shared belief is more unifying than any division, because... | I disagree. These two religions have separate culture, history and practice. They are not the same, because... |

Guru Nanak took some Hindu teachings and some Muslim teachings into the Sikh scriptures. We need that kind of respectful approach to faith: perhaps in the future all religions could merge.

| I agree: the religions are all basically similar, and should link up as much as possible, because... | I disagree: the religions are all unique, each one with its own teaching. They can't all be 'true' because... |

Activity 5 Design a sacred space: if you were spiritual architects...

You have been learning how the Golden Temple expresses Sikh ideas and beliefs about God and humanity. Working with a partner, choose **at least three** from the twelve ideas below, and design a building to express these beliefs. The twelve ideas include several that Sikhs believe in, and others.

Why would people come to your building? Think about how to use steps, doors, water, corridors or causeways, windows, arches and other features.

We believe that God is hard to find.	We believe that there is one God, and truth is his name. He is eternal.	We believe that 'the mouth of a destitute person is the treasure chest of God' (Guru Nanak – a reason to feed the hungry)
We believe that human beings can meet God in silence and stillness.	We believe it is in the family that most spiritual life happens.	We believe that reading ancient wisdom can help human beings today.
We believe that you can be spiritual without being religious.	We believe that music is one of the best ways to find your inner self and spirit.	We believe in being open – to ideas and ways of life from many different religions.
We believe that lots of people find peace, calm, clarity and focus without religion.	We believe there is no God, but human beings can make good use of peaceful community gatherings to seek inner calm.	We believe that if you want to find God or a spiritual path, the best way is to serve other people who are in need.

For your design
1. Make simple drawings of your plan (from above), and the front elevation, on the centre of an A3 sheet.
2. Label your drawings to show the features you have built in, and the beliefs and values they show.
3. Suggest some music, readings, actions and activities, and other ideas that might go on inside the sacred space you have designed.
4. Display your work and see what other students have done.
5. Write an explanation of the main similarities and differences between your design and the Golden Temple. Are they different because of different beliefs, or because of some other variations between you and the Sikhs who built Harmandir Sahib? How do Sikh values of equality and service fit into your plans?

Here are two examples to give you some ideas. Don't look at them unless you are stuck!

'Our design for a spiritual place reflects our beliefs that God is hard to find, that music can make you calm and that reading ancient wisdom and being open is a good way to live. So we have created a building that is like a maze inside, where musical performers and scripture readers can be heard, and where the roof can be rolled back so that you can star gaze while you think spiritual thoughts...'

'We believe that it's in your community with your friends and family that you can be spiritual, because they care for you. We believe that there is 'something out there' but we don't call it 'God'. So our spiritual space is like a restaurant, with circles of seats for people who are close to each other. From the balconies, you can hear scriptures read out loud and music played and sung from many different religions, to make it open hearted.'

HOW AND WHY DO SIKHS REMEMBER GOD?

Summary of learning

The whole of Sikh life, worship and attitudes springs from the fundamental belief in one God who creates, sustains and cares for all. God is to be meditated upon, and worshipped, and from this flows the way in which life should be lived. The example of Guru Nanak and the teaching of the Mool Mantar are both central to this.

Written for **students aged 11–14**, the activities in this section are designed to introduce students to what Sikhs believe about God in a variety of ways which include individual and small group activity, encourage discussion and speculation, and provide opportunity for creative expression.

Information for the teacher

Gurmukh: One who lives by the Guru's teaching.

Guru Granth Sahib: The Sikh sacred scripture.

Gurbani: The writings of the Gurus as found in the Sikh holy scripture, usually specifically those of the Guru Granth Sahib.

Ik Onkar: The opening of the Mool Mantar. 'There is One God'.

Kirtan: Chanting Gurbani, usually to music.

Mool Mantar: Written by Guru Nanak, the Mool Mantar is the basic credal statement of Sikhism. Its focus is the character and nature of God. Also 'Mul Mantar'.

Nam Japna: Repetition of God's name.

Nam Simran: The activity at the heart of Sikh faith – meditating upon the divine name, calling to mind those attributes by which God is revealed to humankind.

Resources

SikhNet Stories for Children
A growing collection of Sikh stories told for young people by Sikh storytellers.
See: www.sikhnet.com/stories

BBC Religion: Sikhism
A comprehensive overview of key aspects of Sikhism.
See: www.bbc.co.uk/religion/religions/sikhism

The Guru Vanishes
The story of Guru Nanak's disappearance in the river told by a Sikh storyteller.
See: http://bbc.in/U4OHjh

CLEO
A collection of short videos developed for RE including a number about aspects of Sikhism.
See: www.cleo.net.uk

Sikhwiki
A searchable encyclopaedia about Sikhism.
See: www.sikhiwiki.org

Outcomes

Students can show their achievements at levels 4–6 through these activities if they can say 'Yes' to some of these 'I can' statements:

Description of achievement:
I can . . .

Level 4

- use the right words to describe what some Sikhs believe about God
- make links between Sikh beliefs about God and how Sikhs might choose to live, giving my own thoughtful comments.

Level 5

- explain the importance of the Mool Mantar for a Sikh and the beliefs about God it expresses
- give my own views about questions to do with religious experience and belief in God, taking account of Sikh beliefs.

Level 6

- use religious concepts and terminology coherently to explain how Sikhs understand and express their beliefs about God.
- express my own insights into Sikh beliefs about God and Guru Nanak's religious experience, raising and addressing philosophical questions.

Learning activities

Activity 1
Guru Nanak experiences God

This activity provides a good way into understanding the origin and nature of Sikh beliefs about God, and the connection of these beliefs to Guru Nanak and the Guru Granth Sahib. It uses story to encourage the skill of speculation and introduces the idea of religious experience.

a Explain that for Sikhs Guru Nanak was the first of the ten human Gurus and that students are going to hear a story about something life-changing that happened to him.

b Tell the story 'Guru Nanak – lost in the river of God' on p.14, pausing at the three points indicated in the text. Ask students to respond to the questions below for each pause point – encourage wide-ranging responses and keep the discussion open-ended.

- **Pause Point 1**

  What do you think Mardana should do?

  What do you think had happened to Guru Nanak?

- **Pause Point 2**

  Why do you think Mardana refused to believe that Guru Nanak had drowned?

  Why do you think Guru Nanak looked different when he came out of the water?

- **Pause Point 3**

  What do you think had happened to Guru Nanak? What sort of experience had he had?

  Why do you think some people thought Guru Nanak was mad?

  What do you think Guru Nanak said when he finally decided to speak?

 For a way of using this story with lower-achieving students, see p.32.

Activity 2
The Mool Mantar

When Guru Nanak finally broke his silence after his experience, one of the first things he said is recorded as the Mool Mantar. These words form the opening of the Guru Granth Sahib.

This spiral text activity uses group work and individual thinking to get students to look carefully at a sacred text.

a Ask students, in pairs or as a class, to suggest words and ideas they associate with people's beliefs about God from their studies in RE. Get them to agree the 'Top 10' beliefs about God.

b Give each group of four an A3 copy of the spiral text activity on p.15, with the Mool Mantar in the centre. Explain that when Guru Nanak came out of the river – these are the words he spoke.

c Students read the Mool Mantar, and then pass the sheets round their group quite quickly (e.g. every two minutes), completing the boxes with their ideas and questions.

Ask probing questions to encourage students to think about their thinking, e.g.

- Why do you say or think that?
- Is there an alternative view?
- What did you learn about Sikh beliefs about God?
- How are they similar or different to the views of other people? And your own?

Activity 3
The importance of the Mool Mantar

The grid on p.16 contains the Mool Mantar, a brief explanation of each phrase and some reflective questions.

Cut the grid up and ask students to match the statement, explanation and questions.

Use the discussion work to set up a written (or oral) piece, taking their learning from Activity 2 a stage further.

Activity 4   Reflecting on Guru Nanak's experience

Now students know what Guru Nanak said after his experience at the river (see Activity 1), talk about what sort of experience they think he had.

Sikhs believe Guru Nanak had a religious experience, where he was in a blissful state and met with God. God revealed the message of the Mool Mantar. After the experience he began his journeys, teaching and setting up Sikh communities.

It must have been an incredible experience, as it inspired Guru Nanak to spend his life passing on the teachings, and it inspires millions of people to follow these teachings. Encourage students to raise questions and consider answers Sikhs might give, and their own responses.

For example, how did Guru Nanak know he had met with God? Could you describe this as a vision or was it something else? How would he know that this was real and not in his imagination? Was it a meeting with a being or as if Guru Nanak had 'merged' into God? Bear in mind the description of God in the Mool Mantar ('Timeless . . . Unborn . . . Self-existent . . .'). How could Guru Nanak describe a 'meeting' with such a being in ordinary words?

Do people have experiences like this today? What would persuade you to follow someone?

Taking it further

An alternative Sikh account, focusing on Guru Nanak's experience more than Mardana's anxiety, can be found at http://www.sikhnet.com/stories/audio/nanak-and-river

Ask students to compare the accounts. What are the similarities and differences? What do we learn about Guru Nanak's experience here?

Story: Guru Nanak: Lost in the river of God

Mardana was sitting on the river bank and waiting. He had one hand on a pile of clothes at his side and across his lap lay his rabab, the musical instrument he played when Guru Nanak, the Master, sang and they worshipped God together.

Early that morning, Mardana had watched Guru Nanak go into the water to bathe as usual. He had waited for him to emerge, before settling into the shade of the big tree to pray.

But this morning there was no sign of Guru Nanak, so Mardana was waiting patiently and trying not to feel anxious.

The following morning, Mardana was still sitting on the riverbank with his hand on the Master's clothes, waiting, afraid to look away from the flowing water, desperate for some movement that would give him hope.

(Pause Point 1)

He had watched the river being searched once the alarm had been raised yesterday. Nothing! The Master must have drowned, they said, but in his heart Mardana refused to believe them. So he sat and waited faithfully.

The next morning, Mardana was *still* waiting, sitting on the riverbank and watching. As the water flowed past him, only his eyes moved. He seemed to have been there for ever.

Suddenly he sprang to his feet and threw his hands up into the air. As he opened his mouth to shout, the sound caught at the back of his throat. What was he seeing? Could he believe it? The Master was calmly walking out of the water, as if he had *just* gone into the river to bathe. As he always did, he was shaking the water from his hair, but his face was more than usually tranquil – it was radiant!

(Pause Point 2)

Mardana truly could not believe what his eyes were seeing, and yet, wasn't this what he had trusted would happen, deep in his heart? Guru Nanak, his beloved friend, was back. What joy! And here he was, dressing again as though it were an ordinary day. Mardana watched him, his head bursting with questions, but each time he opened his mouth to ask, the Master held up his hand as if to silence him, so Mardana had to carry on waiting.

It was many days before the Master spoke. He had continued to wash in the river and then to sit in the shade of the big tree to pray. He had given away all his possessions and some people thought he was mad. A crowd gathered, but he remained silent.

(Pause Point 3)

Activity 2 How do Sikhs describe God? The Mool Mantar

1 Mool Mantar
There is only One God
His Name is Truth
The Creator
Without fear
Without hatred
Timeless
Unborn and self-existent
Known by the grace of the Guru
Guru Granth Sahib, page 1

2 What this means is …

3 A Christian might say …

4 An Atheist might say…

5 What I think about this is …

6 One good thing about this is …

7 One thing I want to ask the writer is …

8 No one's thought of this point yet …

© 2013 RE Today Services
Permission is granted to photocopy this page for use in classroom activities in schools that have purchased this publication.

15

Activity 3 The importance of the Mool Mantar

In pairs, read each line of this grid and talk together about the various questions in column 3.

Mool Mantar	Explanation	Something to think about...
There is only One God	There are different paths to experience the same One God.	There are lots of religions in the world. Talk about some of the similarities and differences you can think of from your RE lessons. Are there any beliefs and practices that are contradictory? Is it possible that all religions lead to the same goal – are all heading to the same God? How do you make sense of that? Sikhs believe this is the case. What difference would that make to the world if they are right?
His name is Truth	Not just all the right answers to questions, but the True One.	How do you feel when you don't know if someone is telling the truth? Can you trust them? How do you feel when someone is being truthful? What difference would it make if someone was always totally truthful? How might this be helpful to Sikhs, to worship the God who is always True?
The Creator	Cause of the universe and everything in it; keeping the universe going, as a dance is kept going by a dancer.	Look at a leaf or a flower. Imagine how pleased you would be if you could make something as simple and beautiful as that! Imagine how clever you would be too! What words might describe a creator of the *world*? How might Sikhs feel about this creator?
Without fear	God has no rivals; nothing can harm or threaten God.	What are you afraid of? Can you imagine not being afraid? What difference would it make to you? Sikhs believe God is not afraid, so how might this help them when they are scared?
Without hatred	God is a good judge, caring and fair.	Do you sometimes get angry? Have you ever been angry with someone else? Does it make you feel good or bad? What would it be like if you could be calm and kind instead of angry and worked up? How might Sikhs be helped by believing God is always calm and kind?
Timeless	Time is the servant of God. God is not tied down by time. God is eternal.	How old are you? How have you changed in the last five years? What will be different about you in five years' time? Sikhs believe that God does not change because time does not affect God. God is just the same, always. What questions puzzle you about this?
Unborn and self-existent	God is free from birth and death. God has not come to earth in a body. God just *is*.	Can you think of something that begins and ends? A piece of music? A day? A year? A seed that grows and dies? A hamster that is born and dies? People? Can you think of anything that does not begin or end? Sikhs say that God is without beginning or end, a being that is not dependent upon anything else. How would that be possible?
Known by the grace of the Guru	You cannot get to God yourself – God must open your eyes. This grace is first offered when you are born a human being.	Who do you know who has 'opened your eyes' to something? How have they done that? Do they just understand it much better than you? For Sikhs, getting to know God is not possible without God's help. In fact, all achievement is a balance of the grace of the Guru and the work of the Sikh. How might a Sikh respond to this?

© 2013 RE Today Services
Permission is granted to photocopy this page for use in classroom activities in schools that have purchased this publication.

RE Today Services

What do young Sikhs have to say about God and worship?

'Guru Nanak taught us that worship is "of the heart". It does not matter what you look like, nor the presence you may have, but having an honest, clean, stable personality matters.

'Always treat people the way you would want to be treated. Always treat people as one family.

'For me, worship at the gurdwara is spiritually relaxing, and you gain a closer sense of belonging to the Sikh faith.'

Parminder, aged 22

'I like the way we worship: it is easy as soon as you get to know it.

'I like Christian worship too – I like the way they sing and pray. Like us, they listen to their holy book being read.

'I hear the words of the Guru at worship, and I feel relaxed, calm and peaceful. I see everyone full of joy and happy. I like it that there's no lying whatsoever in the gurdwara.'

Jaspreet Kaur, aged 13

© David Rose/NATRE

'When I am in the gurdwara, I can hear the Guru Granth Sahib being read, I can smell the incense sticks and I can see people listening. In the langar kitchen, I can taste the food we share, sweet and sugary. I like the fact that Sikhism has no discrimination.

'When I worship, I feel happy, but calm. Maybe God is listening, and understanding what I pray. You don't have to do something extravagant for God to notice you. If it comes from the heart, then you are doing it right.'

Jaipreet, aged 12

'If you talk to God, then when you have done something wrong, you can ask for forgiveness. And one example for me of why worship matters is that when I sat my exams, I was nervous. I would pray before doing them and I felt better.

'When I worship, I feel that God is showing me the right path. I see pictures of Guru Nanak Dev Ji in my mind, and I know he is with me in my heart all the time. I feel grateful.'

Taljinder Khera, aged 15

'I'd like other people to know that we Sikhs worship in a different way to other religions. When I close my eyes to worship, I can see a world full of different cultures, all happy together, not racist.

'I feel glad to be part of my great culture. My religion always makes me feel good inside.'

Amritpreet, aged 12

How do Sikhs remember God?

Activity 5
Nam Simran and Seva

This activity uses the concept of Nam Simran (meditating on God's name) and draws on the perspectives of five young Sikhs to explore the importance of worship for Sikhs and its place in Sikh religious and spiritual life.

a Provide students, working in pairs or small groups, with a copy of the stimulus sheet from p. 17. Ask them to read the quotes and then discuss together and agree:

- six reasons why the young Sikhs like their identity as Sikhs
- five beliefs about God that are found in the quotations
- six reasons why worship is important to them
- five ways in which belief in God affects everyday life.

b Introduce students to Nam Simran – meditating on God's name. Explain that one of the names for God used by Sikhs is **Waheguru** – Wonderful Lord. YouTube is a good source of stimulus for Nam Simran – try the following (and do look at the comments from users – what benefit do they find?): http://bit.ly/TDSwRl

As students listen (for perhaps five minutes), ask them to reflect on:

- The main words used (e.g. Waheguru; Nam)
- The value of repeating and becoming engrossed in, words, phrases and musical themes
- The difference between repeating a word that has been learned (Nam) and repeating words which express something you have experienced and 'know' (Nam Simran). Which is the most important? Why?
- Introduce students to (or remind them of) the Sikh concept of seva – selfless service. Ask students to suggest what is the connection between Nam Simran and seva, and what does it mean in practice.
- Sukhmandir Khalsa has a photo sequence on About.com's Sikhism pages. Use this photo sequence to illustrate seva within the Sikh community: http://bit.ly/wtfxJf
- Ask students to suggest what sorts of activities in the wider community they might expect to see Sikhs getting involved in.

Activity 6
Expressing belief in God

Jaswant Singh Zafar is an engineer by day and a poet, photographer and painter in his spare time. He spent a year in his free time creating paintings on the theme of 'Gurbani'. See this link for a series of oil paintings by Jaswant Singh Zafar weaving the Mool Mantar through a variety of backgrounds: http://bit.ly/Ywu1JO

Ask students to:

a choose one of the paintings and explain its connection to something they have learned about Sikh beliefs about God

b create a work of art of their own to express their understanding of some of the beliefs expressed in the Mool Mantar.

This link to the website of The Singh Twins, internationally known Sikh artists, might provide some inspiration – www.singhtwins.co.uk / http://bit.ly/TFZBjg

The gurdwara is a place for the practice of Nam Simran and Seva.
© David Rose/NATRE

WHAT DO SIKHS BELIEVE ABOUT HOW YOU SHOULD LIVE?

Summary of learning

It is difficult to understand the impact of the teachings of Guru Nanak and his successor Gurus without appreciating the historical and religious context of his time. This unit sets up the context briefly and enables **students aged 11–14** to reflect on reasons for the impact and inspiration of Guru Nanak, using the story of residents of Kartarpur, a community set up by the first Guru.

With an understanding of the background, students can then appreciate the importance of the three core tenets of Sikhism and the practice of the langar, exemplifying the rejection of ritual and the divisions of caste and gender. While issues of caste are still alive within the Sikh community, most Sikhs would see this as cultural and recognise the clear teaching about equality in the Guru Granth Sahib.

This unit explores Sikh morality by asking students to devise and design a board game to show their understanding. By suggesting the Sikh path, through the grace of the Guru, from *haumai* (self-centredness, ego) to *hukam* (living in harmony with the divine will), from *manmukh* (the egoistic individual) to *gurmukh* (the God-centred individual), the game design activity draws together students' understanding of key Sikh practices and teachings.

Using the pages

Learning activities are outlined on p.20. The newspaper resource on p.21 can be used to inform students about Guru Nanak's impact on Kartarpur, or you might prefer to give students the task of producing a front page for themselves, using this example as a model.

The remaining pages support the major activity of devising a board game. This will require several lessons to enable students to produce a high-quality outcome. The temptation for students is to do a basic snakes and ladders game (originally a Hindu game to explore the idea of karma), but this will only show understanding of Sikh teachings if students are explicit about the attitudes and actions that result in progress or regress. The activity does allow for sophisticated responses and some deep engagement with Sikh ways of living.

Activity 3 (p.20) gives a number of ways of following up earlier activities, designed to allow students to demonstrate their learning.

Resources

The following websites give information to support learning:

www.realsikhism.com

www.g5sikhmedia.co.uk

Questions: Ways of Living, an earlier book in this series from RE Today, includes rich resources comparing the lives of two Sikhs, Bhagat Puran Singh who set up the Pingalwara Centre in Amritsar, and Manni Kaur Dulai, who was inspired to serve at Pingalwara.

www.srigranth.org gives a searchable Guru Granth Sahib, including an English translation.

A range of helpful resources are available on the Sikh Missionary Society website (www.gurmat.info/), including an introduction to Sikhism www.tinyurl.com/bcfcsbz

Outcomes

Students can show their achievements at levels 4–7 through these activities if they can say 'Yes' to some of these 'I can' statements:

Description of achievement:
I can . . .

Level 4

- make links between some teachings of Guru Nanak about equality and ways in which Sikhs put these into practice
- refer to some teachings of Guru Nanak to describe how Sikhs have been inspired by their faith to work for equality.

Level 5

- show how the teachings of Guru Nanak had an impact in his time and what impact they have for a Sikh path of life today
- express my views of what Guru Nanak taught about equality, relating his ideas to my life.

Level 6

- show an understanding of how Sikh teachings affect individuals and communities, backing this up with evidence
- express insights into the value of seeking truth and practising community service, relating these to my own life.

Level 7

- show a coherent understanding of Sikh teachings and ways of life
- explain the impact of history and culture on the beginnings of Sikhism
- weigh up the strengths and weakness of the argument that Kartarpur represents an ideal community whose practices should be followed in the UK, using evidence and examples.

Learning activities

Activity 1
Digesting

Help your students to understand the impact of Sikhism at its start, and to reflect on its continuing impact. Use the information about the setting up of the Sikh sangat or community at Kartarpur on p.21. This information has been set out as a newspaper front page, but you can get students to process the information by using one or two of the following suggestions:

a Imagine a DVD telling the story of Guru Nanak and the founding of Sikhism at Kartarpur. Ask students to design a DVD cover with suitable images and a blurb of up to 150 words. This will explain some of the key features of the content and why all should watch it.

b Devise a tourist information guide to attract people to the town. What is there that might appeal, and to whom might the town be most appealing?

c Simplify the information in a format suitable for an 8 year old, to introduce them to Sikhism.

d Conduct some additional research in order to produce a more detailed front page for a broadsheet newspaper.

e Imagine a Hindu Brahmin priest or a Muslim imam reading the *Kartarpur Messenger* at the time. Ask students to imagine what their reaction might be. Guru Nanak welcomed Muslims and Hindus, but not all of them welcomed him; some of his teachings were quite sharp (see the stories on p.21 and p.6).

 A copy of the 'Kartarpur Messenger' may be downloaded by subscribers from the RE Today website.

Activity 2
Devising a game

1 Read the information on p.22 to introduce the activity. Enable students to identify the process from manmukh to gurmukh as the path to liberation, via the grace of the Guru.

2 Give students the information cards from p.23. Ask them to work out which are barriers on the path to mukti, and which actions or attitudes are the ones Sikhism teaches as the right way to live.

3 Read the texts on p.24 and ask students to make any connections they can with the teachings from p.23.

4 Using the cards on p.23, ask students to work in pairs or small groups to come up with one or two specific actions for at least eight of the cards – mixing good and bad deeds – applying the teaching to the everyday life of Sikhs. Note the examples given at the top of p.23.

5 In groups, students should talk about how they might design and set out a game to show a 'path of life' from their learning about Sikhism.

6 Provide time and resources for students to design and produce a game board and instructions. When completed, groups should have a chance to play each other's games and evaluate how well they express Sikh belief and practice.

A good game will show that it is what someone does that should make a difference to their progress, not simply random throws of dice. Similarly, the role of the grace of God in enabling all good actions should be clear.

Activity 3
Deepening learning

Reflection: ask students to write a commentary on their game, to show how it reveals the impact of Sikh teachings on how a Sikh might live.

Application: ask students to consider what their own game for their path of life might be like. Comparing it with the Sikh path, what would be similar, what would be different? Why?

Critical evaluation: 'Kartarpur gives an excellent model for life in a town or city in the UK today.' Do you agree?

Ask students to work in groups to give the strengths and weaknesses of using Kartarpur as a model for towns and cities in the UK. They should use their understanding of Sikh teachings and ways of living from the game activity as well as the information about Kartarpur itself. Can they give good reasons and evidence to back up views both for and against the idea of Kartarpur as a model community? They could present their ideas as a debate or using presentation software.

Personal evaluation: Guru Nanak was a revolutionary in the sense that he spoke out against accepted norms in society with which he did not agree. For example, he openly ate with people of all social backgrounds and faiths in order to emphasise his belief that as human beings we are all equal. This overthrew the notion that some individuals are ritually purer than others as a consequence of the social group that into which they are born. Guru Nanak's actions were not accepted by many individuals around him.

Ask students, working individually: Which aspects of society would they change? How would they go about promoting their ideals? How might they bring change?

As a class, talk about the changes they wish to see. Challenge the class to choose some actions to take to bring change.

CHALLENGE ➤ For some ideas to stretch your higher-achieving students even further, see p.33.

Your news – your views
Kartarpur Messenger

Growing

Since the founding of our wonderful town by Guru Nanak Ji in the year 1522 CE, many people have come to live here from all over the Punjab. Kartarpur means the 'Seat of Kartar' or the 'Seat of the Creator', but it is now also the Seat of the Guru, as Guru Nanak Ji has rested from his travels to dwell here with us!

Seat of the Guru

Guru Ji and his companions, Bhai Mardana and Bhai Duni Chand, inspire us all. They take part in prayers and singing to God. Guru Nanak Ji has set up the community and teaches us the ways of the Divine Guru. He shows us how to live. He has a small farm with his wife and two sons, working hard with his disciples to produce enough to live on. Any extra food he gives to the langar to share with all.

Every day he gets up very early, long before dawn, to meditate, and then gets together with Bhai Mardana for kirtan, singing hymns to God together. All are invited to join in. In the afternoon he teaches all who want to talk with him. Guru Nanak Ji also serves in the langar, collecting water or finding wood for the fire, serving food or sweeping the floor. No person is too high to serve, no service too low for all to practise. He sits and eats with all who come, as all are equal members of one great family: Muslim or Hindu, male or female, rich or poor.

An example

Living this life of a simple householder, Guru Ji shows the true spirit of religion: meditation on the Name of God, service to all and honest living.

'Is ritual useless?'

The Guru keeps on teaching his disciples, helping us all to understand the best way to live. One disciple asked, 'Is ritual useful or useless?'

Guru Nanak answered by talking of his visit to Hardwar, a town nearly 400 miles away by the river Ganges. There were people offering water to their dead relatives who had passed into the next world. They threw handfuls of water towards the sun in the east.

Guru Nanak Ji went into the river and started throwing water towards the west. People laughed at him and asked why he was throwing water in the wrong direction.

Guru Ji's answer was to say that he was watering his crops, withering in his home at Kartarpur in the Punjab. People said he was crazy! 'How can your water reach hundreds of miles away from here?'

'The same way as your water reaches your ancestors in the other world,' Guru Ji replied.

Interviews

We caught up with some of the recent arrivals at Kartarpur.

Ajay says: 'I moved to Kartarpur because I heard that Guru Nanak was living here. I used to live in a village, but life was very hard, as my job (my jati) was to clean toilets. I was an untouchable in my village – outside the caste system. Here in Kartarpur I am raised up to be treated as an equal – no one looks down on me. I can eat with the others in our community kitchen, the langar. I can serve people without polluting them! I serve God and the Guru for this freedom!'

Aisha says: 'I love the fact that I have an equal role as a woman here in Kartarpur. Guru Nanak Ji treats us all with great respect. He says that humanity's future depends upon women, as every person is born from a woman, shaped in a woman's womb. Before I came here, I would not be allowed to play a part in community service. I love it here.'

Baljit says: 'I have heard Guru Nanak teaching: "There is no Hindu, there is no Muslim; I will follow God's path!" That is so simple and yet so difficult! It means that here at Kartarpur we try to put aside differences from our backgrounds. We try to treat each other with respect. We serve each other. We do not have to do lots of rituals to please God. We do not need to go on pilgrimage. We do not need to renounce everything and become holy men, we can stay looking after our families. This is the path to God.'

Sikhi path of life: design challenge!

Design a board game to show a Sikh understanding of life

Design a board game that shows a path of life for a Sikh person. Use the information below to help set up your game.

Include good and bad actions and attitudes from the resource sheet on p.23.

Show which ones are obstacles and which ones help a Sikh to get close to God and mukti.

Design the layout and include instructions to show how to play the game.

- Sikhi teaches that human life is a gift from God, Waheguru.
- The path of life from birth to death gives human beings a chance to move from being self-centred (manmukh) to being God-centred (gurmukh), overcoming the ego (haumai) through living according to the will of God (hukam). In such a state, one can escape the cycle of life, death and rebirth (samsara) and achieve liberation (mukti).
- Mukti is a state of indescribable bliss, where the God-centred person (gurmukh) merges with God.
- Achieving mukti is the result of living a life tuned to the will of God, remembering the Creator (nam simran) and performing seva, selfless service to others.
- Lots of things can get in the way of a Sikh achieving this – temptations and vices are obstacles.
- Lots of actions can help a Sikh make progress – internal attitudes as well as practical actions.
- The path depends both on human effort and divine will. The human being is not a puppet and so needs to take action. However, no progress can be made without Divine Grace (gur prashad).
- Sikhi teaches that humans do not only live once. Through transmigration of the soul we need many chances to learn how to get close to God.
- Like a spark from a flame, the human soul is a flicker of God-light that comes forth from God and returns to God.

What kind of game?

o You might think about a pathway game with dice; squares with good actions allow you to move forward or along a shortcut; squares with bad actions holding you up, or sending you backwards.

o You might think about a snakes and ladders game, but be specific about what attitudes/actions move you up the ladders and down the snakes.

o You might have a multi-layer game, where different levels represent different lives in the cycle of life, death and rebirth.

Sikhi path of life information file

- Use the following resources to set up your game.
- Where is the start and where is the goal? Where will these go on your board game?
- You must decide which of the attitudes and actions described here are good or bad. Which attitudes and actions will help a Sikh to reach God? Which ones will prevent them?
- Give some specific examples, e.g. wash up at the langar (helpful action); go on pilgrimage (no value to such rituals); not bother to work for your exams (unhelpful action); aim to get as much money and stuff as possible (unhelpful action); be boastful about your achievements (unhelpful attitude).

Repeating the name of God, Waheguru, to develop self-control when facing difficulties.	The grace of the Guru (gur prashad). All good deeds are only possible through God's grace.	Work hard for your boss, earning enough money to live on (kirt karo).	Pride: put yourself first; don't worry about other people. It's survival of the fittest in this world.
There is so much fantastic stuff in the world; be greedy to hang on to it. It's easier than seeking truth.	Work hard to prepare for your exams (kirt karo) and earn an honest day's living.	Stop worrying about your fears and submit to the will of God to bring contentment.	The path of life from birth to death gives humans a chance to move from being self-centred (manmukh) to being God-centred (gurmukh).
You should believe in caste and treat some people as better or worse than others.	Patience: be strong-willed and kind-hearted.	Lust can distract you. It stops you meditating and becoming one with God. It is a wound of the soul.	Escape the cycle of life, death and rebirth (samsara) and achieve mukti, liberation.
Truthful living: your thoughts, words and actions should all match up.	Let your anger build within you; you are right and everyone else is wrong. Of course you should rage at them!	*Vand ke chakko*: share your food and earnings with the less fortunate.	Life is short, everything is temporary, so cling on to worldly attachments. You will lose them soon enough when you die.
Rituals are of no value in reaching God; God is within you.	You should overcome the ego (haumai) by living according to the will of God (hukam).	Justice: respect the rights of others and give equal opportunities to all.	Serve others equally: there is no rich, no poor, no black or white, no male or female: all are equal before God.
Becoming a God-centred person is a process of transformation, like butter being churned from milk. It takes effort.	Mukti is a state of indescribable bliss, where the God-centred person (gurmukh) merges with God.	Life is a search for truth, reaching out beyond the finite to the infinite perfection of God.	Becoming amritdhari is an important step on the way to serving the Guru and your fellow human beings.

Sikhi: a path to God

Here are some teachings from the Guru Granth Sahib (or Adi Granth – AG). The number refers to the page in the Adi Granth. The Japji Sahib is a hymn, AG 1-8, written by Guru Nanak and recited as part of morning prayers.

Use the teachings from the Guru Granth Sahib to help as you plan your board game. Make any connections that you can with the ideas on p.23.

The man who is in tatters but is full of the love of God gains a good reputation, but a life of luxury is worthless when it becomes all-absorbing. *Guru Arjan, AG 745*	As fragrance dwells in a flower or the reflection in a mirror, so does God exist in all. Then why not seek God in your heart? *Guru Tegh Bahadur, AG 684*	We do not become saints or sinners by just saying that we are; it is the actions that are recorded on the soul. According to the seed we sow, is the fruit we reap. By the Grace of God, O Nanak, man must either be saved or continue the cycle of births. *Guru Nanak AG 4 (Japji)*
Those who work hard and share their honest earnings with others, Nanak, they alone tread the true path. *Guru Nanak, AG 1245*	Where there is 'I', 'You' (God) are not. Now there is 'You', and 'I' has vanished. *Devotee Ravidas, AG 657*	People utter the name of God with their lips but bliss dawns only when it fills their hearts. *Guru Amar Das AG 491*
The more a Sikh becomes in tune with the Creator, 'God and a devotee become as close as a fish is to water and there is no distance between them.' *Guru Arjan Dev, AG 1278*	For success in any task, seek first the grace of God. He will grant you success. *Guru Ram Das, AG 91*	Give up those tasks in which there is no value, otherwise in the Court of the Divine Guru, you will feel humiliated! *Sheik Farid, AG 1381*
Truth is foremost, but higher than truth is truthful living. *Guru Nanak AG 62*	Wealth is a she-serpent, it clings to the whole world. She consumes whoever serves her. *Guru Amar Das, AG 510*	Why do you behave as though this body is permanent? It passes like the dream in the night. Whatever you see, it is sure to pass away like the shadow of a moving cloud. Nanak! They who know this world is impermanent seek protection in the name of the Lord. *Guru Tegh Bahadur, AG 219*

WHAT DOES IT MEAN TO BE A YOUNG SIKH IN BRITAIN TODAY?

Summary of learning

It is important that RE lessons give students an encounter with religious faith as it is lived. This unit for **students aged 11–14** includes interviews with some young British Sikhs, talking about the impact of their faith. Pages 27–9 include interviews and related activities. Pages 30–1 give the resources for a mystery, a thinking skills activity exploring a real-life issue faced by some Sikh students. The resources and activities enable students to consider the challenges and benefits of having a religious faith in Britain today.

Useful websites

www.ewfc.co.uk

This site provides information for schools in response to questions about religious beliefs and practices. The Sikh section provides advice to schools for when students become khalsa Sikhs.

Two **contemporary Sikh blogs** are rich sources of information about the Sikh community.

See: www.kaurista.com and www.thelangarhall.com/

Information for the teacher

Sikhi: Currently there is much discussion among Sikhs as to whether the suffix of *ism* should be applied when referring to the Sikh faith. This stems from narratives relating to the understanding that the Sikh faith is a dharma, a way of life. Hence many Sikhs would prefer to refer to their faith as Sikhi, rather than Sikhism.

Amritdhari/khalsa Sikh

An amritdhari Sikh is one who has been initiated into the Khalsa. They will wear the 5Ks, although not all who wear a turban and the 5Ks are amritdhari (initiated). Many Sikhs are *kesdhari* (do not cut their hair or beard) without necessarily being amritdhari. There are also significant numbers of Sikhs who cut their hair and may be labelled as *mona* or *sahajdhari*.

When talking about becoming amritdhari, the terms baptised/baptism should be avoided since they have Christian connotations; instead initiated/initiation should be used.

Outcomes

Students can demonstrate achievement at levels 4–6 in these activities if they can say yes to some of these 'I can' statements:

Description of achievement:
I can . . .

Level 4

- describe how taking amrit will have an impact on a Sikh teenager
- make links with Sikh practices and explain how my way of life reflects my own beliefs and values.

Level 5

- explain why Sikhs see taking amrit as a serious commitment, and how it has an impact on the Sikh community
- compare Sikh initiation with ways in which I make my own commitments, giving similarities and differences.

Level 6

- show that I understand why Sikhs express their commitment differently, using the example of wearing the kirpan
- explain why having a religious faith may be both a challenge and a support in Britain today, giving my own thoughtful response.

© David Rose/NATRE

© RE Today Services

Learning activities

Activity 1
Learning about British Sikh life through the words of young people

Copy the three quotation sheets from pp.27–9. The activities on each page get progressively more demanding, so you can decide who gets which sheet. Students should work in pairs.

There are a series of key pieces of vocabulary used in the quotations. For example *amritdhari* and *khalsa Sikh* both refer to someone who has taken part in the amrit ceremony and now wears the 5Ks, promising to take on additional spiritual practices and to make additional promises of commitment to the beliefs and values of Sikhism. You may wish to have a series of definitions of these terms or have a suitable source available for the students to find definitions for themselves.

After students have completed their sheet(s), run a group or class discussion to share ideas, questions, perceptions and answers.

Activity 2
Deepening learning about commitment

Ask students to research the practice of taking amrit. They can use the information learned from Activity 1, and clip 3780 and 3781 from the BBC Learning Zone website. Ask students to show their understanding by answering these questions:

- Why might a Sikh choose to take part in the amrit ceremony?
- How do Sikhs promise to live their life once they have become an amritdhari or khalsa Sikh?
- How are Sikhs regarded who are not khalsa Sikhs?

Activity 3
Should Gurjit remove her kirpan in school? A thinking skills activity

This 'Mystery' thinking skills strategy provides a structure through which students can:

- **sort** relevant from irrelevant information
- **interpret** information
- **make** links between different pieces of information
- **speculate** to form hypotheses
- **check, refine** and **explain**
- **talk about** their learning and thinking processes.

Copy pp.30-1 onto card and cut up to provide enough sets of cards for students working in groups of four.

Explain to students that they need to:

- **work together using the information on the cards to find an answer** to the central question (there is not necessarily a right answer)
- **sort** through the clues in their set of cards, and **decide** whether they contribute to an answer to the question
- use the cards as they **discuss, decide, explain, prioritise and refine** their thinking
- **share** with the whole class their answer to the question and **justify** their reasons.

Activity 4
Evaluating the arguments

a Ask students to use their learning from the interviews and the mystery activity to produce a balanced, two-sided opinion piece for the local newspaper, giving a range of arguments for both sides. This gives them an opportunity to clarify different viewpoints.

b Imagine that Gurjit is asked to speak to the school student council to present her case. Get students to prepare and present her arguments. Note that this presentation will be quite different in tone from the newspaper activity – it will be passionate, persuasive and personal.

c Ask each student to imagine s/he is the member of the School Council. What is their decision and why? They must weigh up the different viewpoints and say which arguments are strongest.

Activity 5
The challenge of living with faith

Set students the following essay title or debate theme:

'It is an advantage to have a religious faith in the twenty-first century.'

Students should show that they have thought about different points of view and built on their learning about young British Sikhs from this unit. They need to consider the challenges and benefits of living with a religious faith.

© David Rose/NATRE

Identity and belief: how does being a Sikh affect how you live your life each day?

It affects my life a lot; it makes me a better person, a better human being. It's taught me many life lessons. For example, never judge someone by their mistakes as every human being makes mistakes.

Being a Sikh makes me live my life with pride, to know that I belong to something so special and unique. It also makes me work hard in what I do and it influences me to use my strengths.

It's never really made me behave differently to my non Sikh friends, neither has it drawn us apart. My religion teaches me that the whole human race is one family and that the light of God is within every single human being: no one is superior or inferior.

Inderpal, 15

Being a Sikh makes me more careful and wary of the things I do as I believe things I do could influence what people think about the whole Sikh community so I try to stick to the straight and narrow.

It has made me behave very differently to my friends as lots of my friends have been influenced by alcohol, smoking and even drugs. Being a Sikh and following the teachings of the Guru Granth Sahib I have to refrain from doing such things. I have to admit this is hard as it is the popular thing to do, but at the end of the day Guru Ji is more important to me than popularity.

Manjeevan, 16

I believe that everyone is equal just like Guru Nanak Dev Ji taught and that everyone is entitled to hold their own opinions and to follow whichever religion they wish to because there is only one God who is seen in many different forms. For example, Muslims follow Muhammad, Christians believe in Jesus, some Hindus may believe in Goddess Lakshmi and Sikhs believe in Sri Guru Granth Sahib Ji. We all believe in someone who has taught many followers about what is right and what is wrong. To be honest, most of the teachings are similar in all religions.

Harpreet, 14

I don't think I could have been anywhere near what I am today if I didn't have my faith and religion to turn to whenever I was in need of mental and emotional support. I know that no matter what happens, Waheguru (God) will always be there to put me out of my despair. I have uncut hair which teaches me to be mentally strong and not to give up on things, no matter what. This encourages us to develop strength inside ourselves, which is why I believe I am able to stand up to any challenges I may face.

Being a Sikh has had a big impact in the way I behave when around my non Sikh friends. This is because Sikhism teaches us to respect all religions and faiths; and treat everybody equally, no matter what race they belong to. As a result, whenever my friends inform me of any religious activities they are participating in, I encourage them with all my heart and support them with it as it is their complete right to do so.

No matter who is involved in some sort of argument (my friend or not), I believe that I should always stand up for the person I believe is doing the right thing. This won't be in an aggressive way but in an extremely friendly way, I would peacefully explain my opinions to the person and allow them to understand the cause of the argument.

Mehak, 16

1. Read the four quotations aloud with your partner. Which ones do you find surprising? Interesting? Puzzling? Why?
2. List four similarities and three differences you notice between these four young Sikhs.
3. What questions would you like to ask each of the Sikh young people here? How might they reply?
4. Show that you understand what matters to these Sikhs by writing the entries for their Year Book at the end of their school career. Use the headings: Most likely to be . . . Least likely to be . . . Most likely to say . . . Least likely to say . . . and explain your comments.
5. Imagine you were asked for quotation about how your beliefs and values affected the way you live your life – how would you answer? Write a quote to be used by 11–14 year olds about how your beliefs and values affect how you live your everyday life. Write this in about 100 words.

Identity and commitment: Will you become an amritdhari Sikh?

I have thought about it and have decided I definitely want to at some stage in my life, maybe not anytime now as I'm not ready. I believe I still need to learn more and become closer to my Guru, but I will definitely be making my footsteps towards it. Khalsa Sikhs influence me so much and one day, in the future, I would love to become a khalsa Sikh.

If I find it difficult to decide to make the commitment, I assume I'm not ready yet. Becoming a khalsa Sikh is a very big commitment and it's a decision I will not take lightly. I will only take this step when I truly have that thirst to become a khalsa Sikh.

I guess the thing that would be difficult is sustaining the lifestyle and discipline daily. It will make me very proud and feel like I'm officially a part of something great. It will help me stay on track in my journey to becoming one with God.

Inderpal, 15

I have thought about becoming a khalsa Sikh and wearing the 5Ks. I don't think it would be difficult wearing the 5Ks. The benefits are that we are showing we are Sikhs and proud. It helps us to stick out from the crowd. The hard thing for me would be getting up for Amrit Vela (a time for prayer and meditation 2½ hours before sunrise!) and reading the different Gurbanis at the correct times. These are extracts from the Guru Granth Sahib to be read at specific times of the day.

Manjeevan, 16

I wish to take amrit in the future, with my husband when I get married, and after I have children. This is so I will have enough time to be able to follow all the rules and regulations. I hope that until I become a khalsa Sikh I will follow the path of Sikhi and follow the rules and regulations. I know though that life is short and that I may not even live tomorrow. That's why I decided to follow the path of a khalsa Sikh but not become one yet. Once I wear all the 5Ks I will feel like I have a huge responsibility on me but hopefully that wouldn't affect me negatively.

Harpreet, 14

I have always been fascinated with the idea of becoming a full khalsa Sikh and wearing all the 5Ks. In the future, when I feel like I can honestly keep up with the requirements of becoming one, I would definitely love to accept the full form of Sikhi.

This will be a very difficult decision for me. I come from a family who are extremely religious yet not amritdhari. They follow every teaching wholeheartedly and do a lot of seva for the community.

It is important that I feel spiritually and physically ready for it. As it is a big step, I don't want to end up disrespecting the values of being amritdhari. I want to make sure that before I make any decision, I am already being able to follow every little guideline set out by Guruji. However, if I do wear all the 5Ks one day, the biggest benefit I will receive is that I will feel extremely proud of myself within. I know that I will have that eternal happiness inside me because of it.

Mehak, 16

1. Read each quotation aloud with your partner. From each writer, identify one benefit and one challenge of becoming a khalsa Sikh.
2. Write a list of five things that the young people suggest a khalsa Sikh will need to do or not do. Which of these do you think would be the easiest for them, and which the most difficult? Why?
3. Find four pieces of evidence that becoming a khalsa Sikh is a serious step. Explain why you think it is serious for these young people, and why some are hesitating before taking amrit.
4. Why do you think each of the young Sikhs might decide to become a khalsa Sikh in the future?
5. Write a balanced account about the challenges and benefits of being a khalsa Sikh.
6. What kinds of decisions do you face that require this kind of careful thought? Why will you need to think so carefully? How will you make your decision? Is there anything you can learn from these Sikh young people?

Values and commitments: What do you think Sikhism can teach the wider community?

I think Sikhism can teach the wider community to lead happy lives with fulfilment. It can teach the community to become better human beings and to treat each other equally and have unity within the community.

It can also inspire individuals to do amazing things. Sikhism can teach people to remember God, serve people selflessly, not to judge anyone as no one is perfect, to stand up to injustice and oppression, and not forget to make one's mind sharp with the greatest weapon of all – knowledge.

Inderpal, 15

I believe Sikhism can teach the wider community to show love and affection for everyone and not only their own race or religion. It also shows that you should stand up for everyone's rights and not just your own, as well as teaching that everyone is equal regardless of gender, caste, creed or colour.

Manjeevan, 16

Sikhi can teach
- how to maintain an appropriate lifestyle that will allow one to gain actual inner peace
- how to deal with problems that may occur in one's life
- how everyone should love each other for who they are as humans.

Sikhi teaches the core things that every human being should have: love, humanity, equality and humility. This religion also teaches the fact that both men and women are equal and therefore they both should be treated in the same manner and with the same respect.

Harpreet, 14

Sikhism as a whole can teach the wider community an uncountable amount of things. The three principles of Sikhism 'naam japo', 'kirt karo' and 'vand ke chhako' can summarise all these teachings.

- *naam japo* means meditation on the name of God – no matter what religion you are, have faith and remember his name at all times
- *kirt karo* means working hard – whatever work you do, work as hard as you can to gain a successful outcome
- *vand ke chakko* means sharing – you should share your earnings and what you have with the ones who are in need before thinking about yourself; to consume as a community and consider others before yourself.

I believe that these three principles of Sikhism are the basis of life and can teach the wider community all that is needed to become a good human being.

Mehak, 16

1. Read the four quotations aloud with your partner. Use a highlighter or underlining to pick out the values, wisdom or ideas that these young Sikhs think Sikhism can offer to the wider community. There are more than ten.
2. Choose ten of these and, working with your partner, rank them in order of importance. Compare your list with another pair and discuss any disagreements.
3. Choose three of the ideas and write a paragraph about each, explaining why this value, piece of wisdom or idea is significant to a Sikh and then why it might be useful or not useful to a non-Sikh.
4. Why do these Sikhs think society needs to learn these lessons? Imagine that the government have asked for ideas on how to make our country a better, happier place. Write two letters to a local MP, one of them as if from a Sikh viewpoint (using the ideas above) and one from your own viewpoint, explaining what is necessary to make the UK a better, happier place. (If you are Sikh, write a second letter from a different viewpoint.)

Should Gurjit remove her kirpan in school?

Gurjit is an amritdhari or khalsa Sikh. She took amrit at the age of 14. Khalsa Sikhs should wear the 5Ks.	After moving house Gurjit now attends a school in a small town which only has a small Sikh community.
Gurjit used to go to a school in the middle of the city. The school had students of lots of different religions and had a description of acceptable kirpans.	Her old school rules said the kirpan should be: fitted with a strap to stop it being withdrawn; no more than 15 cm long, the blade no more than 7.5 cm long; worn under clothes; never displayed openly to ensure safety at all times.
Gurjit is hoping to become a vet when she leaves school.	When Gurjit decided to become a khalsa Sikh, she and her family spoke to her old school and made arrangements for her to wear the 5Ks in school and store them appropriately during PE.
The 5Ks are: *kesh* – uncut hair; *kangha* – a comb to keep the hair tidy; *kara* – a steel bracelet; *kaccha* – shorts to be worn under clothes; and the *kirpan* – a small sheathed ceremonial sword worn under clothes.	An amritdhari or khalsa Sikh promises to wear the 5Ks and makes other promises to become more committed to living up to the expectations of the Gurus.
Schools in areas with lots of Sikh pupils work with the community to find a way to let Sikh students wear the 5Ks in school.	School rules state that no jewellery can be worn in school and no offensive weapons may be brought into school.

Kirpan comes from *kirpa* – 'mercy and kindness' and from *aan* – 'honour and dignity'.	The Criminal Justice Act 1988, which deals with carrying articles with points or blades, gives an exemption if the person is carrying the item for religious reasons.
Gurjit loves to play hockey. At her old school she played for the Under 16 team.	Some Sikhs wear a small kirpan around their neck.
When travelling through security at airports, khalsa Sikhs are expected to remove their kirpans.	Gurjit's new school have told her they will not allow her to come to school wearing a kirpan.
There is only one secondary school in the small town that Gurjit and her family have moved to.	In 1699, Guru Gobind Singh, the final living Sikh guru, said that khalsa Sikhs should wear the kirpan at all times.
Gurjit is the first person to become an amritdhari or khalsa Sikh at the school. There are no Sikh members of staff at the school.	It was a difficult decision for Gurjit to become a khalsa Sikh. She thought for a long time about whether she would be able complete the spiritual practices and follow the path of the Gurus.

ACCESS

Three ways to make the learning in this book more accessible for lower-achieving students.

Visual learning: the Golden Temple

The visual learning section of the book (pp.5–11) is already accessible to most students. For those with special needs, ask a classroom assistant to work with a small group.

Better questioning: Take three or more pictures (photos or works of art) and print them for students to compare. Ask them to look at each picture and say four things about it they don't know. These become questions:

- 'I don't know where this is.' 'Where is the Golden Temple?'
- 'I don't know what is inside.' 'How can you find out what's in the Golden Temple?'

Lower-achieving students develop simple questioning skills like this. As a group, can they use an information book, or the pages in this book, to find some answers?

Draw and label: students either draw their own image of the Golden Temple on an A3 page, and label it, or they use a picture, stuck in the centre of the page, and label this. Alternatively, they could match labels provided by the teacher, stick them on the page, and draw lines that connect them to the feature of the Golden Temple they describe.

Illustrating a story: Guru Nanak lost in the River of God

The story on p.14 is central to Sikh understanding of how the religion began. Get a group of ten to make a class picture book. Tell them it is for children half their age to learn the story – so must be simple and colourful.

Put the ten sentences below on to card. Read the story from p.14 together, and get students to sequence the cards. If each student draws a picture to go with one of these sentences, they can be put together in a class book.

1. Guru Nanak went into the river to bathe every morning.
2. His friend Mardana would wait on the riverbank for him to finish washing.
3. One morning Guru Nanak did not come out of the water. Mardana was scared.
4. Lots of people from the village came to search the river and banks to find Guru Nanak.
5. Some people said 'we will only find his body now'.
6. Three days passed and Mardana was full of grief. He still sat on the river bank.
7. Guru Nanak stepped up out of the river water, shaking the drops off his beard.
8. Guru Nanak's face was full of peace and full of light.
9. Mardana could not believe his eyes. How could the Master be standing there, dripping?
10. Guru Nanak gave away all his things to poor people.

Ask the students to think about whether there should be two or three more pages, to show what happened next. The 'early finishers' could do another page agreed by the group.

A bit of a rap

One strand that runs through the whole of Sikh teaching is about human equality. Show this text to small groups, and see if they like it, or want to write a better one of their own. Can they work together to perform it as a rap or chant? Can they add some more verses?

Doesn't matter if you're short
Doesn't matter if you're tall
Doesn't matter if you're big or small
The Guru says we're all equal.

Doesn't matter if you're black
Doesn't matter if you're white
Doesn't matter if your race is mixed
The Guru says we're all equal.

Doesn't matter if you're posh
Doesn't matter if you're poor
Doesn't matter if you're in between
The Guru says we're all equal.

Doesn't matter if you drive a Porsche
Doesn't matter if you ride a bike
Doesn't matter if you always walk
The Guru says we're all equal.

Doesn't matter if your mum's the queen
Doesn't matter if you dad's a cleaner
Doesn't matter if you're fat or lean
Equal's what the Guru says we all are! Every one. No exceptions.

 An audio/mp3 file example of the rap may be downloaded by subscribers from the RE Today website.